Golf Jokes For Ladies

The Ultimate Collection of Golfing Jokes for Ladies

By Charlotte Croker

Jokes for Lady Golfers

This is quite simply the best collection of the very best golfing jokes for ladies ever produced.

Written by a woman, for women, this joke book is free of any sexist jokes.

There are some great one-liner golf jokes, plenty of questions and answers themed golf gags, many story led jokes which are designed to be easy to remember, a few risqué golf stories too, some clever golf sayings and all in all, there is something for everyone.

This mixture of golfing jokes is guaranteed to get you laughing and will prove that female golfers have a good sense of humor.

Published by Glowworm Press
7 Nuffield Way
Abingdon OX14 1RL

FOREWORD

When I was approached to write a foreword to this book I was very flattered.

That is until I was told that I was the last resort by the author, Charlotte Croker, and that everyone else he had asked had said they couldn't do it!

I have known Charlotte for a number of years and being able to create funny jokes is a trait of her family.

I remember her once telling me that to see something really funny, I should just watch her short game.

She is quick witted and loves creating clever puns and amusing gags and I feel she is the ideal person to put together a golfing joke book just for women.

She will be glad you have bought this book, as she has an expensive lifestyle to maintain.

Enjoy!

Major Mulligan

Table of Contents

Chapter 1: Golfing One-Liners

The game of golf is 90 percent mental and 10 percent mental.

If you think it's hard to meet new people, just pick up the wrong ball on a golf course.

Golf is an easy game that is just hard to play.

You know you're a hacker when your divot goes further than your ball.

Definition of the game of golf:

A five-mile walk punctuated with disappointments.

A husband walked into the bedroom and found his wife in bed with her golf clubs. Seeing the astonished look on his face, she calmly said, "Well, you said I had to choose."

I played a round of golf today and I had two good drives. To and from the golf club in my car.

Golf is a game in which the slowest people in the world are those in front of you, and the fastest are those behind.

I really like the 19th hole. It's the only place I can drink after I drive.

No, I did not lose my ball.

I know where it is - it is in the middle of the lake.

Did you hear about the cross eyed assistant pro who got sacked because he couldn't see eye to eye with the female members?

My doctor told me to play 18 holes a day, so I went to the shops and bought a harmonica.

My husband complained about my obsession with golf. I asked him if it was driving a wedge between us.

Fairway: [faer-wai]: A tract of closely mown grass running directly from tee to the green. Your ball can usually be found to the left or right of it.

I golf in the low 90s.

I don't play if it's any hotter than that.

Did you hear about the Scotsman who gave up golf after playing for twenty years? He lost his ball.

My game is so bad I had to have my ball retriever re-gripped.

The reason the pro tells you to keep your head down is so you can't see him laughing.

Good golf etiquette: Always concede the fourth putt.

I didn't miss the putt; the ball missed the hole.

What are the three rules of golf? (1) If the ball goes right it's a slice. (2) If the ball goes left it's a hook. (3) If the ball goes straight it's a miracle.

Our minister is a very good golfer. Mind you, he's had lots of practise in keeping his head down.

Definition of an oxymoron: An easy par three.

I am divorcing my husband because he simply doesn't understand golf at all. He even thinks Tiger Woods is a forest in India.

There is no shot in golf that is so simple that it can't be messed up.

A golf widow's lament: - "When I die, I would like to be buried on the golf course so I know that my husband will visit me."

Ladies who say that a shank is close to a perfect shot have never had two in a row.

A woman goes to a clairvoyant, who tells her, "I see lots of sand, trees and water. You must be a golfer."

I seldom make the same mistake twice in golf. But then again, I seldom do anything twice in golf.

I enjoy shooting in the 100's. I figure I'm getting more for my money.

Golf is a frustrating game.

Yesterday, I was just two strokes away from a hole in one.

Chapter 2: Question and Answer Gags

Q: Why is the game called 'golf"?

A: *Because all the other four letter words were already taken.*

Q: How are golf balls like eggs?

A: *They are white, they are sold by the dozen and a month later you have to buy more.*

Q: What do golf and sex have in common?

A: *They're two things you can enjoy even if your husband isn't very good at either of them.*

Q: What's the difference between a golf ball and directions?

A: *A man will ask for help looking for a golf ball.*

Q: What's the difference between golfers and the general population?

A: *Fewer people have reached 100.*

Q: What's the easiest shot in golf?

A: *Your fourth putt.*

Q: What are the four worst words you could hear during a game of golf?

A: *It's still your turn.*

Q: What do you call the perfect golf shot?

A: *A fluke.*

Chapter 3: Shorter Golfing Jokes

You can easily change the names in here to suit your own story telling purposes.

Carla tells her friend off saying, "You're late on the tee, Gabrielle."

Gabrielle replies, "I am sorry, but as it's a Sunday, I had to toss a coin to see if I should go to church or go and play golf."

Carla says, "Okay, but why are you so late?"

Gabrielle replies, "I had to toss the coin five times."

A mixed foursome is on the first tee.

"It's raining a little today," the husband stated. "You and I aren't bothered by a little rain, are we?"

"Why is he telling you not to be bothered by a little rain?" the other woman said to his wife.

"He's not talking to me," the wife replied, "He's talking to his golf bag."

"Sometimes my husband fades the ball, sometimes he draws it," one wife said to another as they waited to tee off.

"How does he decide which shot to play?" said the other wife.

"It depends," his wife replied as her husband hit the ball into the rough on the left of the hole.

"That was a draw," she told her friend.

She continued, "If he wanted to be in the rough on the right side of the hole, then he would have faded it."

Amanda stood over her tee shot for a very long time; looking up, looking down, looking left, looking right, wiggling her legs, double checking the distance, figuring the wind speed and direction.

Finally her frustrated partner asks, "What's taking you so long?"

Amanda answers, "My husband is up there watching me from the clubhouse. I want to make this a perfect shot."

Her partner says, "Forget it. You don't stand a snowball's chance in hell of hitting him from here!"

Alison said to Sally, "I discovered something really important about golf today. I discovered that I really should study the marker that is posted by the tee box very carefully."

Sally asked, "Does that help you choose the right club to play?"

Alison replied, "No, it helps me play the right hole."

Four female golfers were introducing themselves to one another on the first tee.

One asked, "How do you feel about a lot of swearing and moaning?"

"It doesn't bother me at all," answered another.

"Great," replied the golfer who had asked the question. "In which case would you like to telephone my husband and tell him where I am."

It's a foggy day, and two dim-witted ladies are teeing off on a par 3. They both tee off, and walk up to the green to find their balls.

One ball is about four feet from the cup while the other has found its way into the cup for a hole-in-one. Both were playing the same type of ball and also the same number, Taylor Made 4, but they couldn't determine which ball was which, and which one of them had made the hole in one.

They decided to ask the golf pro to help out.

After congratulating both ladies on their fine shots, the golf pro asks, "Which one of you used the orange ball?"

I was asked, "Has your swing changed much over the years?"

I replied, "It hasn't changed much, but it sure has changed often."

A lady is on the first tee - a long par 3 over water and the pro advises her to hit a brand new Titleist Pro V1.

The lady tees up the Titleist and takes a couple of practice swings.

The pro says to him, "On second thoughts, hit a range ball."

Two ladies are talking in the bar after their round.

Jenny asks, "You made a 9 on a par 3? How did you manage that?"

Wendy replies, "I chipped in from the fringe."

"Do you pay a high price to play golf here?" a lady golfer was asked as she left the club house.

"I will today." the golfer replied "I didn't tell my husband that I was coming here."

Two men were putting on the fourteenth green, when a pair of ladies played up just short of the green.

As the men teed off on the next hole, they noticed the ladies quickly chip on and putt out, before walking very quickly up to their tee.

Sensing their bafflement, one of the ladies said, "Sorry, do you mind if I play through - I've just heard that my husband has had a terrible accident and I need to get home urgently."

A golf professional was approached by two women in the pro shop.

"Do you wish to learn to play golf, madam?" he asked one of the ladies.

Oh, no," she replied, "it's my friend who's interested in learning. I learned last Thursday."

A couple is at the altar on his wedding day. By their side are the man's golf bag and clubs.

His bride asks, "What are your golf clubs doing here?"

The groom replies, "Well this isn't going to take all day, is it?"

Sally sliced her drive into a field of chickens alongside the 3rd hole, striking one of the hens and killing it instantly. She was understandably upset, and went to see the farmer.

"I'm very sorry," she told him, "my dreadful tee-shot hit one of your hens and killed it. Can I replace the hen?"

"I doubt it," replied the farmer, contemplating the situation. "How many eggs a day do you lay?"

It is pouring with rain and two lady golfers are standing on a tee box overlooking a river, and are getting ready to hit their tee shots.

One of them points up the river, turns to the other and says, "Just look at those chumps out there fishing in this rain."

An Irish lady is on vacation in Florida and after her round she goes into the clubhouse.

The head pro says, "Did you enjoy it out there?"

She replied, "It was marvelous."

The pro asked, "Just how did you find the greens?"

The Irish woman replied, "Quite easy. I just walked to the end of the fairways and there they were."

Two lady golfers are in the bar after a round of golf.

Madison tells Karen, "I was one under three times today."

Karen asks, "What do you mean?"

Madison replies, "Well, I was one under a bush, one under a tree and one under a cart."

A husband complains to his wife, "You spend so much time thinking about golf. Do you even remember our last wedding anniversary?"

The wife replies, "Of course, I do darling. It was the same day I sank that 70 foot putt."

A husband and wife go to a marriage counselor as they are having problems with their marriage.

The counselor asks them what the problem is and the wife lists every problem they have had in the twenty years they've been married, and she is very detailed.

After listening for ten minutes the counselor decides it's time for action, so he stands up, walks around the desk and embraces the woman, kissing her passionately.

The woman is taken aback and after the long kiss, she sits down quietly in a daze.

The counselor turns to the husband and says, "That is what your wife needs at least three times a week, can you do that?"

The husband says, "No I can't. We play golf together on Mondays and Fridays, but I can bring her in for you on Wednesdays."

Two golfers are in the bar after a round of golf.

Zoe, the better of the two golfers says, "I played World War II golf today - out in 39 and back in 45."

No to be outdone, Lucy says, "I played Civil War golf today - out in 61 and back in 65."

Two golfers are ready to play on the 12th tee as a funeral cortege passes by.

Nora doffs her cap, and bows her head as the cortege passes by.

"That was a really nice thing to do," her good friend Alice says. "It's good to see there is still some respect in the world."

"Well, it's only right," Nora replies. "I was married to him for 30 years."

Emilia hit her ball deep into the trees.

There was a 'whack, whack, whack' over and over again, until finally she got the ball out.

Her playing partner asked, "How many strokes did it take you to get out of there?"

Emilia replied, "Four."

Her partner then said, "I heard eight."

Emilia explained, "Four of them were echoes."

A husband complains to his golf mad wife, "I'm tired of your obsession with golf."

The wife replies, "Why? Is it driving a wedge between us?"

On a visit to the fortune teller the lady captain asks, "Are there golf courses in Heaven?"

The fortune teller replies, "I have some good news, and I have some bad news."

The lady captain asked, "So what's the good news?"

The fortune teller said, "The good news is that Heaven's golf courses are gorgeous and far better than anything you could imagine."

The lady captain asked, "What's the bad news?"

The fortune teller replied, "You have a tee-time at 9:30a.m next Tuesday morning."

Ruby and Lydia are playing a challenging course and Ruby is struggling with her tee shots.

On the 7th hole she hits a huge slice.

She asks Lydia, "Did you see where that ball went? Is it in the deep rough?"

Lydia replies, "Yes it is."

Ruby asks, "How far in?"

Lydia replies, "A long way in. I just hope our cart has 4-wheel drive."

An alien spaceship silently hovered over a golf course and the aliens inside watched a pair of female golfers in complete bewilderment.

One of them topped her tee shot, sliced her second into the deep rough, took four shots to get her ball out of the rough back onto the fairway, shanked the next shot into the bushes, and she then took three more shots to get it out on the fairway again.

She then thinned the ball into a bunker, and took several more shots to get out of the bunker onto the green.

She putted four times until she finally got the ball into the hole.

At this point, one alien said to another, "Wow, now she is in serious trouble."

A junior golfer was questioning low handicapper and club legend Evelyn Thomas.

The young woman said, "You are a great golfer. You really know your way around the course. What is your secret?"

Evelyn replied, "It's simple. The holes are numbered."

A group of four lady golfers were on the tee of the 401 yards par 4 sixteenth hole.

There was a road that ran alongside the hole on the left hand side.

The first golfer teed off and hooked her tee shot into the road where it bounced 150 yards down the road, until it hit the tire of a moving bus and was knocked back onto the golf course stopping just 10 yards short of the green.

As they all stood in amazement, a fellow golfer asked, "How on earth did you manage to do that?"

The response came without hesitation, "You just have to know the bus schedule."

Madeline was playing a round of golf with the club pro one day and after a few holes she asked the pro, "What do you think of my game?"

The pro replied, "You should shorten your clubs by two inches."

Madeline asked, "Do you think that would help my game?"

The pro replied, "No, but it will help them fit in the trash can."

Two women were put together as partners in the club tournament and met on the putting green for the first time.

After introductions, the first golfer asked the other, "What's your handicap?"

"Oh, I'm a scratch golfer," the other replied.

"Really?" exclaimed the first woman, suitably impressed that she was paired up with her.

The other woman replied, "Yes, I write down all my good scores and scratch out the bad ones!"

Two ladies were enjoying a club match, when after a bad shot on the first hole, the younger lady of the two heard the older lady mutter, 'Hoover' under her breath.

On the second hole, the older lady's ball went into a water hazard and she said, 'Hoover' again, a little louder this time.

On the third hole, her putt edged the hole rather than going in, and once again she said, 'Hoover.'

The younger lady asked, "Just why do you say, 'Hoover' after a bad shot."

The older lady replied, "It's the biggest dam I know."

Andrea and Clara were getting ready to tee off on the first hole when Clara noticed that Andrea had a new set of irons.

Clara asked Andrea if she liked her clubs and if they had helped her game.

Andrea replied, "They're great clubs. They've added at least 10 yards to my slices, about 15 yards to my hooks and you would be amazed at the size of my divots now."

Olivia and Sophie are playing a course they had not played before, which came with a reputation for being really hard.

Sophie teed up on the first hole, addressed the ball, took a couple of waggles and took a swing.

She hit a foot behind the ball, made a huge divot and totally missed the ball.

Unphased she stepped back, took another couple of practice swings, addressed her ball, swung, missed everything and took yet another huge divot.

She stepped back from her ball and said to Olivia, "This is a really tough course."

A lady comes home after her regular Tuesday golf game and her husband asks her why she doesn't play with Paula Lewis any more.

The wife said, "Well, would you want to play with a woman who regularly cheats, swears up a storm over everything, lies about her score, and has nothing good to say about anyone, ever?"

"Of course I wouldn't," replies the husband.

"Well," says the wife, "neither does Paula Lewis."

One sunny afternoon, a single lady was added to a couple's golf game.

After a few holes the couple asked her why she was playing alone.

She explained that she and her husband had played this course every year for 20 years, but this year he had died and she wanted to keep the tradition going in his honor.

The emotional couple wondered if there were any friends or family who would have liked to play with her today.

She replied, "I asked myself that same question, but they all preferred to go to the funeral."

A young lady and a priest are playing together.

At a short par 3 the priest asks, "What are you going to use on this hole?"

The young lady says, "An eight iron, Father. How about you?"

The priest says, "I'm going to hit a soft seven iron and pray."

The lady hits her eight iron and her ball lands on the green.

It is the priest's turn, but he tops his seven iron and the ball dribbles into the greenside bunker.

The young lady says, "I don't know about you, Father, but in my church, when I pray, I keep my head down."

A woman goes into her local newspaper office to get an obituary for her recently deceased husband published.

The obituary editor informs her that there is a charge of a dollar per word.

She pauses, reflects, and then says, "Well then, let it read 'Steve Daniels died.'"

The editor tells her that there is a seven word minimum for all obituaries.

She thinks it over and then says, "In that case, let it read, 'Steve Daniels died: golf clubs for sale.'"

A man and his wife walked into a dentist's office.

The woman said to the dentist, "I am in a hurry. I have two friends waiting to play golf with me. I just don't have time to wait for the anesthetic to work. So let's forget about the anesthetic and just pull the tooth and be done with it."

The dentist thought to himself, "My goodness, this is a very brave woman, asking me to pull her tooth without using anything to kill the pain."

So the dentist asked her, "Which tooth is it, Madam?"

The woman turned to her husband and said, "Open your mouth, darling, and show the dentist which tooth hurts."

A priest was halfway down the seventh fairway, waiting to hit his second shot, when he heard a shout of "Fore!" just before a ball slammed into his back.

The flustered golfer who had hit the ball was soon on the scene to offer her apologies.

When the priest assured her that he was all right, the woman smiled.

"Thank goodness, Father," she exclaimed. "I've been playing this game for fifteen years, and I have finally hit my first holy one."

A forty-something single enthusiastic lady golfer was browsing an online dating site called Singles247.com when she came across an interesting profile from a handsome man living just twenty miles away.

The profile read as follows - Slim, attractive, brunette, 5' 7", successful in business, happy in life, good sense of humor, no children (or desire to have them), enjoys traveling and the finer things in life. Seeks similar qualities in a partner for long term relationship. Golfers need NOT apply.

The wife told her husband, "My doctor just advised me to give up golf."

Her husband asks, "Why? Did he look at your dodgy shoulder?"

The wife replies, "No, he looked at my scorecard."

Two couples went out golfing together.

The men teed off first, and one of the guys took a huge swing at the ball, missing it completely, while passing some gas rather loudly in the process.

No one commented.

He addressed the ball once more but this time he passed just a little gas as he made contact with the ball, topping it and moving it only a short distance.

He said, "I wonder why the ball didn't go very far."

His wife said, "I don't think you gave it enough gas."

A young female golfer was at her first golf lesson when she asked the pro, "Is the word spelled put or putt?"

The pro replied, "P-U-T means to place something where you want it whereas P-U-T-T means a futile attempt to do the same thing."

A newly wed man said to his new wife, "Honey, now that we are married, I would like you to play golf once a week instead of twice."

She said, "You are beginning to sound like my ex-husband.

He said, "I didn't know you were married before."

She replied, "I wasn't!"

Veronica hooked her tee shot deep into a wooded ravine on the fourteenth hole.

She took her nine iron and clambered down in search of her ball.

After many minutes of hacking at the undergrowth, she spotted something glistening in the leaves.

As he got closer, he discovered a skeleton with a nine iron in its hands.

Veronica immediately called out to her partner, "Aubrey, I've got a major problem down here."

"What's the matter?" Aubrey asked from the edge of the ravine.

Veronica replied, "Bring me my wedge. You can't get out of here with a nine iron."

Eileen is not the brightest individual in the world.

One day she popped into the Pro shop to see if she could get a bargain.

The assistant pro showed her a set of clubs, and said, "These clubs will cut your handicap by 50%."

Eileen replied, "That sounds like a good deal. I'll take two sets."

Four old friends met on Tuesday morning for a round of golf.

One gasped, "These hills get steeper as the years go by."

The second spluttered, "The rough seem to be getting longer."

The third complained, "The greens seem to be getting smaller."

The fourth, the wisest of the group, said, "Let's all be thankful that we're still on this side of the grass."

Chapter 4: Longer Golfer Jokes

The names used in this book are the products of the author's imagination or used in a fictitious manner. Any resemblance to actual persons, living or dead is purely coincidental.

Of course, you can easily change any of the names to suit your own story telling purposes.

Heart Attack

A husband and wife are on the twelfth green when suddenly he collapses from a heart attack.

"Help me dear," he groans to his wife.

The wife ran off saying, "I'll go and get some help."

A little while later she returned; picked up her putter and began to line up her putt.

Her husband raises his head off the green, glares at her and says, "I'm dying and you're putting?"

"Don't worry dear," says the wife calmly, "I found a cardiologist on the seventh hole and he's on his way to help you."

"How long will it take for him to get here?" he weakly asks.

"Not long, darling," says his wife. "Everybody has already agreed to let him play through."

The Witty Golfer

After a particularly poor round of golf, Sarah skipped the 19th hole and was walking towards her car when a policeman stopped him and asked, "Did you tee off on the sixteenth hole about twenty minutes ago?"

"Yes," Sarah responded.

The cop asked, "Did you happen to hook your ball so that it went over the trees and off the course?"

"Yes, I did. How did you know that?" she asked.

"Well," said the policeman, "Your ball flew out onto the road and crashed through a driver's windshield. The car went out of control and crashed into a fire truck."

The policeman continued, "The fire truck couldn't make it to the fire, and the building burned down. All that because you hooked a tee shot. So, what are you going to do about it?"

Sarah replied, "I think I'll close my stance a little bit, tighten my grip and lower my right thumb."

The Hospital Visit

A man staggered into a hospital with concussion, multiple bruises, a black eye, and a five iron wrapped tightly around his throat.

The doctor asked him, "What happened to you?"

The bruised guy replied, "Well, I was playing a round of golf with my wife, when at a difficult hole, she sliced her ball into a cow pasture. We went to look for it and while I was looking around I noticed one of the cows had something white at its rear end."

He continued, "I walked over, lifted its tail, and sure enough, there was a golf ball with my wife's monogram on it - stuck right in the middle of the cow's butt."

"I held the cow's tail up and I yelled to my wife, 'Hey Honey, this looks like yours.'"

"I don't remember much after that."

Hitting Over A Tree

A lady is having a playing lesson with the old professional at her golf club.

When they reach the 14th fairway, the lady is facing a difficult shot. A large birch tree is in front of her ball, directly between her and the green.

After a little time pondering how to hit the shot, the pro says, "You know, when I was your age, I'd hit the ball right over that tree."

The lady realizes the pro has just laid down the gauntlet, so she decides to try and hit her ball over the tree, rather than play safely to the side of it.

She swings hard, hits the ball, and watches it fly into the branches, rattle around a bit, and then land at the foot of the tree.

"Of course," says the pro, "when I was your age, that tree was only three feet tall."

The Deaf Mute

A woman about to tee off was approached by a man who held out a card that read, "I am a deaf mute. May I please play through?"

The lady gave the card back, and shaking her head, said, "No, you CANNOT play through."

She assumed that the deaf mute was able to lip read so she mouthed, "I can't believe you would try to use your incapacity to your own advantage like that. Shame on you."

The deaf man walked away and the lady continued to play her round.

On the next hole, just as she was addressing her approach shot to the green, she was hit in the head by a golf ball that knocked her out cold.

When she came to a few minutes later, she looked around and saw the deaf mute sternly looking at her, with one hand on his hip, and the other hand holding up four fingers.

The Incredible Golf Ball

Two ladies were about to tee off when one of them noticed that her partner had only one golf ball.

She asked, "Don't you have at least one other golf ball?"

The other lady replied that she only needed one.

"Are you sure?" the friend persisted. "What happens if you lose that ball?"

The other lady replied, "This is a very special golf ball. I will not lose it so I don't need another one."

The friend asked, "What happens if you hit it into the trees and it gets lost among the bushes and shrubs?"

The other lady replied, "That's okay. You see, this special golf ball has a homing beacon. I'll be able to find it - no problem at all."

"Well," the friend asked, "what happens if the ball goes into a lake?"

"That's okay too," she replied, "this special golf ball floats. I'll be able to retrieve it."

Infuriated, the friend asks, "Okay. Let's say our game runs late, the sun has gone down, and you hit your ball into a sand trap. What are you going to do then?"

No problem," says the other lady, "this ball glow in the dark. I'll be able to see no problem at all."

Impressed, her friend asks, "Where did you get a golf ball like that anyway?"

The other lady replies, "I found it."

Unlucky Golfer

Lady Luck was seldom kind to Samantha. Although she had a real zest for life she was constantly beset by bad luck.

She was unlucky in love many times and her life seemed to be full of more downs than ups.

Her greatest delight was her golf game. Not that Samantha was a good golfer; in fact, she rarely managed to break 100.

Eventually Samantha became ill and passed away. In her Will, she requested that her remains be cremated and her ashes be scattered on the fairway on the seventh hole of her home course.

After the funeral service, a gathering assembled to carry out Samantha's wishes. It was a bright sunny day and all was going well. Then, as the ashes were being strewn, a gust of wind came up and blew poor old unlucky Samantha out of bounds.

Double Trouble

Teresa had just completed a rough divorce and to clear her mind went to play a round of golf.

While waiting on the first tee, she reached into the trash can and pulled out a rusty lamp. She rubbed it to get the dirt off and lo and behold a genie popped out. The genie told the woman that he would grant her three wishes, under the condition that her ex-husband would get double what she wished for.

Teresa agreed, and said she wanted a Tesla. The genie reminded her that her ex-husband would get two of them. She said she didn't mind as long as she had one for herself. Poof! The genie said it was done.

Her next wish was a million dollars in the back of her Tesla. The genie reminded her that her ex-husband would receive 2 million. Teresa said she didn't care and told the genie to fulfill the wish. Poof! The genie said it was done.

She thought long and hard for her final wish. She then handed the genie her 5-iron and said calmly, "Beat me half to death."

Lightning Strike

Emily and her partners were desperately trying to finish their round before the predicted thunder and lightning arrived.

Although rushing, she was playing a fantastic round, and she decided to stay on the course although the weather was getting worse.

On the 16th hole she sliced her drive into the trees, as the thunderstorm came in.

She found her ball in an OK lie and decided to chip back onto the fairway. However, as she took her club to the top of her backswing, lightning struck down from the sky catching her steel shafted 9 iron.

Her friends hurried over only to see a crater in the ground and no sign of Emily or her clubs - she was gone.

When she reached the Pearly Gates, Saint Peter said, "We are very sorry to have taken you at such an early age, but as you love the game, and you had the round of your life going, we decided to bring your clubs that you love so dearly with you so that you can play all the courses of heaven which are more incredible than any golf course that you have ever played."

The woman started crying, to which Saint Peter said, "I know, you have left behind many loved ones."

Emily said, "No, that's not it."

St. Peter said, "Yes my son, you also had an unbelievable life and a great career."

"No, that's not it either," sobbed Emily.

St. Peter said, "Well then, what could make you so unhappy, that you would cry so much?"

Emily looked up as the tears flooded from her eyes and replied, "I think I left my wedge next to the 14th green."

Play The Ball Where It Lies

Two good friends, Barbara and Mandy, were playing golf one day.

Barbara was a stickler for the rules and always insisted that they adhere strictly to the rule about not improving a lie.

After a few holes, Mandy's ball landed on a cart path.

As she reached down to pick up her ball to get relief Barbara said, "You can't do that – you cannot improve your lie."

No matter how much Mandy tried to explain she was entitled to free relief, Barbara would simply not allow it.

So Mandy went over to the cart to get a club.

She stood over the ball and took quite a few practice swings, each time scraping the club on the cart path, sending out lots of sparks.

Finally, after several practice swings she took her shot. The ball flew straight and landed on the green about eight feet from the pin.

"Great shot," Barbara exclaimed. "What club did you use?"

"YOUR 6 iron." Mandy replied.

Ship High In Transit

In the 17th century, most products were transported by ship and it was also before the invention of commercial fertilizer, so large shipments of manure were common.

It was shipped dry, because it weighed less but once water hit it, fermentation began which produced methane gas as a by-product.

The manure was stored in bundles below deck and once wet with sea water, methane began to build up.

If someone came below decks at night with a lantern, then it would often ignite the methane, and there would often be a huge explosion.

Several ships were destroyed in this manner before the cause of the explosions was determined.

Afterwards, the bundles of manure were stamped with the term "Ship High In Transit" which directed the crew to stow it in the upper decks so that any water that came into the hold would not reach this volatile cargo and produce the explosive gas.

Thus evolved the term "S.H.I.T" (**S**hip **H**igh **I**n **T**ransit) which has come down through the centuries and is still in use today.

You probably did not know the true history of this word.

Neither did I. I always thought it was a golf term.

The Ducks

Three golfing buddies died in a car crash and went to heaven.

Upon arrival, they saw the most beautiful golf course they have ever seen. St. Peter told them they were welcome to play the course, but he warned, "Do not step on the ducks under any circumstances."

The men had blank expressions on their faces, and one of them queried, "The ducks?"

"Yes," St. Peter said. "There are thousands of ducks walking around the golf course, and when one of them is stepped on, he squawks, and then the one next to him squawks, and so on, and it makes an awful noise which breaks the tranquility. So, if you step on a duck, you will be severely punished."

The men start playing the course, and after just a few holes, one of the guys stepped on a duck. The duck squawked, and soon there was a cacophony of noise with countless other ducks quacking.

St. Peter then appeared on the scene with an ugly woman and asked, "Who stepped on a duck?"

"I did," admitted one of the men.

St. Peter immediately pulled out a pair of handcuffs and cuffed the man to the plain woman. "I told you not to step on the ducks," he said. "Now you'll be handcuffed together for eternity."

The two other men were now extra cautious not to step on any ducks, but a couple of weeks later, one of them accidentally did. The quacks were as deafening as before, and within minutes, St. Peter walked up with a ugly woman again. He determined who had stepped on the duck by seeing the fear in the man's face, and he cuffed him to the woman.

"I told you not to step on the ducks," St. Peter said. "Now you'll be handcuffed together for eternity."

The third man was now even more careful. After three months golfing, he still hadn't stepped on a duck.

Then, out of the blue, St. Peter walked up to the man with the most beautiful woman the man had ever seen. St. Peter smiled and without a word, handcuffed him to the beautiful woman and walked off.

The man, knowing that he would be handcuffed to this woman for eternity, let out a sigh and said, "What have I done to deserve this?"

The woman replied, "I don't know about you, but I stepped on a duck."

The Lost City

For months the archaeologists had been toiling deep in the jungle, clearing creepers and choking undergrowth from the faint traces of a Lost City.

Their excitement mounted as the site's extraordinary purpose became evident. There were long wide streets of giant cobblestones with small circular holes every few hundred yards.

It simply had to be...a golf course!

Any doubt was dispelled by the discovery of sculptures and paintings of human figures using primitive prototypes of golf clubs.

The next step was to interrogate the local tribesmen about the traditions associated with the prehistoric golf club of the Lost City. It was soon learned that the tribal leaders did indeed have legends of the Old Ones who followed a weekly ritual using primitive clubs and balls, until they were overcome by tragedy.

Via an interpreter, a professor asked, "If only we knew why they gave up golf, making it vanish for centuries before rediscovery."

The tribal elder, surprised, made a sweeping gesture and replied.

"Simple," was the translation, "they could not afford the green fees."

Slow Group

The same group of lady golfers played every Tuesday afternoon at 1pm. They were known as the TAG Society and they always finished their rounds by 5pm so they could have a good gossip and enjoy a bottle or two of wine together.

One Tuesday, they ran into a very very slow four-ball ahead of them. The ladies in the TAG Society waved at the group in front many times, but the group ahead did not move aside to let the ladies through.

After a frustrating five hours round, the ladies came into the bar fuming. The slow group was at a table across the room and the whole bar could hear the swearing coming from the TAGs.

Eventually, a waitress approached the TAGs and said, "You ladies should calm down. That group you're cursing? They can't see. They're blind golfers and let's face it, it's great they can even play."

One of the TAG group felt terrible and said to the others, "The waitress is right. Tell you what, we should send them over a bottle of Chardonnay on our tab."

Another one in the group said, "That's a good idea, but let's send them a bottle of Sauvignon instead."

Everyone looked at the leader of the group for her to approve.

"Sod them," she grumbled, "Tell those idiots to play at night."

How Many?

Juliet and Ann were two of the bitterest rivals at the club. Neither woman trusted the other's arithmetic.

One day they were playing a heated match and they were watching each other like hawks.

After holing out on the fifteenth green and marking a six on the scorecard, Juliet asked Ann, "What did you have?"

Ann went through the motions of mentally counting up her shots.

"Six," she exclaimed and then hastily corrected herself, "No, no....a five."

Calmly Juliet marked the scorecard, saying out loud, "Eight."

"Eight?" Ann said, "I couldn't possibly have had eight."

Juliet said, "Well, you claimed six, then changed it to five, but actually you had seven."

"Then why are you marking down eight?" asked Ann.

Juliet told her, "It's a one stroke penalty for improving your lie."

A Good Golfer

Diane brings a friend along to play golf with two of her regular partners.

Her buddies ask if here friend is a good golfer and Diane replies, "She's very good."

On the first hole, Diane's friend hits her tee shot into the trees.

Her regular partners look at Diane and say, "We thought your friend was supposed to be a good golfer."

Diane replies, "Just watch, she will recover. She's a very good golfer."

They then saw the ball fly out of the trees onto the green where the new girl took two putts and made par.

On the second hole, she hits the ball into a lake.

Her regular partners look at Diane and say, "We thought your friend was supposed to be a good golfer."

Diane replies, "Just watch, she will recover."

The new girl walked into the lake. Two minutes pass and there's no sign of her. Suddenly, an outstretched hand comes out of the water and Diane's buddies tell her to dive in to save her drowning friend.

Diane replied, "You don't understand, that just means she wants a 5 iron."

Hole In One

Paula had been playing golf for over twenty five years but never had a hole-in-one.

On day, as she was walking along a fairway, she said out loud, "I'd give anything to get a hole-in-one."

"Would you give up half your sex life?" came a voice from behind.

Startled, Paula turned around to see a small grinning, red-clad figure with horns and a tail.

"Yes, Yes I would." Paula replied.

"It's a deal then." said the horned figure who then disappeared.

On the very next hole Paula's tee shot looked good the moment she hit it, with the ball running into the hole for her first ever hole-in-one.

Paula was the happiest she had ever been on a golf course, and as she was yelling with joy, she noticed that the little horned figure in red had re-appeared and was standing beside her on the tee-box.

"Now for our bargain," the horned figure said. "You remember you must give up half your sex life."

Paula frowned and said, "Yes I do, but that causes me a problem."

"Don't back out of this," cried the figure. "We struck a deal and you agreed to it."

Paula replied, "Yes, of course. But which half of my sex life do you want - the thinking or the dreaming?"

Imaginary Balls

Two lady golfers are paired together as they share the same psychological problem.

They both have the same doctor who has prescribed a game of golf for them and he has instructed them both to play with an imaginary golf ball to reduce their stress levels.

After a day of splitting fairways and getting many pars and birdies with their imaginary balls, they reach the 18th hole.

The first one tees off with her imaginary ball and she declares, "Look at that beautiful shot – look it has finished just on the edge of the green."

The second lady then hits her imaginary ball and indicates that it has also landed on the edge of the green, and next to the other ball.

They walk up to the green and the first lady takes aim with a 30-foot putt.

She then exclaims, "How about that? My ball rolled into the cup. I win the match."

The second lady responds, "Unlucky. You just hit my ball by mistake. You thus forfeit the hole, and the match!"

The Genie In The Bottle

A young married couple are playing golf, when the wife has a wild tee shot, which flies off into a nearby villa, breaking a dreadful crashing sound.

The young couple decide to investigate, so they go up to the beautiful villa and they knock on the door.

Hearing no answer and noticing the door is open, they go inside.

Entering the villa they notice a golf ball and an ancient broken bottle near a broken window.

Out of the blue a distinguished middle-aged gentleman introduces himself to them saying, "Much gratitude for freeing me. I have been trapped in that bottle for two thousand years, and now I can grant three wishes for releasing me: I will grant you one wish each, but the third is up to me."

The husband declares, "I want a Ferrari."

His wife then says, "I want a wardrobe full of designer dresses."

They hear the reply, "So be it."

He continues, "My desire is to have sex with the lady present here. After two thousand years of abstinence, I hope you understand."

The husband and wife agree to it since their extravagant wishes had been granted.

So the wife goes upstairs for a lengthy sex session.

Lying in bed afterwards, the woman is asked, "How old are you and your husband?"

She replies breathlessly, "We're both thirty two years old, but why do you ask?"

He says, "Well, you would think by now you would have stopped believing in genies."

Four Sons

Four women were due to play golf, and three had arrived and while they were waiting on the fourth to show up they started discussing their children.

The first woman told the others how her son had started out as a used car salesman, and he now owned a car dealership and was doing so well, that last year he gave a friend a brand new car as a present.

The second woman said that her son has his own construction firm having started work as a bricklayer and that he's doing so well that last year he was able to give a good friend of his a brand-new house.

The third woman boasted that her son had worked his way up through a stock trading company, and is now so successful that just last month he gave a close friend of his a large amount of shares in Microsoft as a gift.

As the fourth woman joins them, the other three women inform her that they have been discussing how successful their respective sons are, and are curious to find out how her son is getting on.

She tells them, "Actually I'm unhappy with the way my son has turned out. He has been a hairdresser for many years, and he recently announced to me that he is gay. However, he must be good at what he does, because his last three boyfriends have given him a car, a brand new house and some shares in Microsoft."

Loudspeaker Announcement

An elderly gentleman was addressing the ball when an announcement came over the loud-speaker, "Will the gentleman on hole number one please not hit from the Ladies' tee box."

The old guy backs away, a little distracted, then approaches his ball again. As he does, there is another announcement over the loud-speaker, "Will the gentleman on hole number one please not hit from the Ladies' tee box."

The old man is now annoyed and after backing away from his shot, approaches his ball one more time. This time the announcement came, "We need the gentleman on hole number one to move off the Ladies' tee box."

The old timer turns around and angrily yells, "I need the announcer to shut up and let me play my second shot."

Religious Golf

Jesus and Saint Peter are golfing.

Saint Peter steps up to the first hole, a short par four, and he hits the ball long and straight, and it finishes just short of the green.

Jesus is up next and he slices his ball and it heads over the fence into traffic on an adjacent road.

The ball bounces off a car, onto the roof of a house and into the rain gutter, down the drain spout and onto a lily pad at the edge of a lake. A frog then jumps up and snatches the ball in his mouth. As he does, an eagle swoops down and grabs the frog in its talons. As the eagle flies over the green, the frog croaks and drops the ball into the hole.

Saint Peter looks at Jesus, exasperated.

"Are you going to play golf properly?" he asks "Or are you just going to muck around?"

Agony Aunt

Dear Deirdre,

I desperately need your advice. I have suspected for some time that my husband has been cheating on me. He has been going out with "the guys" a lot recently and when I ask who they are, he always says, "Some friends from work."

On these nights out, I try to stay awake to look out for him coming home, but I usually fall asleep. Anyway, I have never approached the subject with him as I think deep down I don't want to know the truth, but last night he went out again and I decided to check up on him when he got back. Around midnight, I decided to hide in the garage behind my golf clubs so I could get a good view of when he arrived home from his night out with "the guys."

While crouching behind my clubs I noticed that the graphite shaft on my driver appeared to have a hairline crack by the club head.

Is this something that can be fixed or should I go and buy a new driver?

Signed,

Confused

Confession

A woman goes to confession one Sunday and says, "Forgive me father for I have sinned."

The priest asks if she would like to confess her sins and she replies that she used the 'F-word' over the weekend.

The priest says, "Just say three Hail Marys and try to watch your language."

The woman replies that she would like to confess as to why she said the 'F-word.'

The priest sighs and tells her to continue.

She says, "Well father I played golf on Sunday with my friend instead of going to church."

The priest says, "And you got upset over that and swore?"

The woman replied, "No, that wasn't why I swore. On the first tee I sliced my drive into the trees."

The priest said, "Is that when you swore?"

The woman replied, "No, it wasn't. When I walked up the fairway, I noticed that my ball must have had a lucky bounce and I had a clear shot to the green. However, before I could hit the ball, a squirrel ran by and grabbed my ball and scurried up a tree with it."

The priest asked, "Is that when you said the 'F-word'?"

The woman replied, "No, because an eagle then flew by and picked up the squirrel in its talons and flew away."

The priest let out a breath and queried, "Is that when you swore?"

The woman replied, "No, because the eagle flew over the green and the dying squirrel let go of my golf ball and it landed 9 inches from the hole."

The priest screamed, "Don't tell me you missed the f*cking putt."

Frank Discussion

A husband and wife are lying quietly in bed reading when the husband looks over at his wife and asks her a question.

Husband: "Would you get married again if I died?"

Wife: "Definitely not, honey."

Husband: "Why not? Don't you like being married?"

Wife: "Of course I do."

Husband: "Then why wouldn't you remarry?"

Wife: "Okay, yes, I would get married again."

Husband: "Would you live in our house?"

Wife: "Sure - it's a great house."

Husband: "Would you sleep with him in our bed?"

Wife: "Where else would we sleep, honey?"

Husband: "Would you replace my pictures with his?"

Wife: "That would seem like the right thing to do."

Husband: "Would you play golf with him?"

Wife: "Yes - Those are always good times."

Husband: "Would he use my clubs?"

Wife: "'No, he's left-handed."

Silence.

Wife: "Oh Damn!"

Arm Transplant

A keen male golfer was involved in a horrible car crash and was rushed to hospital.

"I have some good news and some bad news for you," the surgeon told him. "The bad news is that I will need to remove your right arm."

"Oh God no, my golfing days are over," cries the man. "So what is the good news?"

The surgeon replies, "The good news is that we have another arm available to replace it with, but it's a woman's arm so I will need your permission before I can go ahead with the transplant."

The man says, "As long as I can play golf again, you have my permission."

The operation went well and a year later the man went in for a check-up.

"How's the new arm?" asks the surgeon.

"Just great," says the golfer. "I'm playing the best golf of my life. My new arm has a much finer touch, and my putting has really improved."

"Not only that," continued the golfer, "my handwriting has improved, I've learned how to sew my own clothes and I've even taken up painting landscapes in watercolors."

Chapter 5: Rude Golfing Jokes

If you feel you will be offended by rude jokes, you'd best skip this chapter.

A husband walked into the bedroom and found his wife in bed with her golf clubs.

Seeing the surprised look on his face, she calmly said, "Well, you said I had to choose."

Q: How do you know a golfer is cheating on his wife?

A: He puts his driver in the wrong bag.

Q: What is the difference between a lost golf ball and the G-spot?

A: A man will happily spend three minutes looking for a lost golf ball.

A married couple played golf together every day.

One day the man and his wife were on the third hole of their local course. He was ahead on the left of the fairway watching his wife hit her three wood.

She hit the ball cleanly; but unfortunately, it hit her husband smack in the back of the head killing him instantly.

There was an inquest into the man's death, and the coroner said it was clear how he died, in that he was killed by a golf ball, and that there was a perfect imprint of a Pinnacle 2 golf ball on the back of his head.

The wife said, "Yes, that was my ball."

The coroner then went on to say that he was a bit concerned to find a Pinnacle 3 ball inserted up the man's backside, and could the wife throw some light on this?

The wife replied, "Oh that must have been my provisional. I wondered where that ball went."

Paula and Andrea are being held up by two men who are playing terribly slowly in front of them.

Finally, after watching the men in the distance as they lined up their putts for what seemed like an eternity, Andrea decided to do something.

"I'll walk ahead and ask them if we can play through," Andrea said.

She set off down the fairway, walking towards the men. But when she got close to them, she stopped, turned around and headed back to where Paula waited.

"I just can't do it," Andrea said, sounding embarrassed. "One of them is my husband and the other is my mistress."

"OK," Paula said, "I'll go and ask them then."

She started up the fairway, only to stop halfway and turn back.

"What's wrong?" Andrea asked when Paula returned.

Paula replied, "Small world, isn't it?"

A couple are playing in the annual Husband and Wife Club Championship.

They are playing in a play-off hole and it is down to a 6 inch putt that the wife has to make.

Unfortunately, she misses the putt and they lose the match.

On the way home in the car the husband angrily says to his wife, "I can't believe you missed that putt. That putt was no longer than my 'willy'."

The wife looked at her husband, smiled and said, "Yes honey, but it was much harder."

A grandfather was at his granddaughter's wedding reception, giving her advice on having a happy marriage and a great life.

The young bride asked, "Grandfather, what's it like making love when you reach your age?"

The grandfather replied, "Well, it's kind of like putting with a rope."

Two women were playing golf. One teed off and watched in horror as her ball headed directly toward a group of men playing the next hole. The ball hit one of the men. He immediately clasped his hands together at his groin, fell to the ground and rolled around in agony.

The woman rushed up, and immediately began to apologize.

She said, "Please let me help. I'm a physical therapist and I know I could relieve your pain if you'd allow me."

"Oh, no, I'll be all right. I'll be fine in a few minutes," the man replied.

It was obvious that he was in agony, lying in the fetal position, still holding his hands together at his groin.

The female golfer urged him to let him help him, so at her persistence, he allowed her to help.

She gently took his hands away and laid them to his side, loosened his trousers and put her hands inside. She administered tender and artful gentle massage to his privates.

Five minutes later the man was sighing with satisfaction when she asked, "How does that feel?"

He replied, "That feels great, but it's actually my left-hand thumb that really hurts."

Maria and Roberta were enjoying a round of golf.

Roberta had putted out at the ninth green and had walked back to the cart. As Maria sank her putt, Roberta sat on a bee and got a very nasty sting and suddenly jumped out of the cart and lowered her panties. She desperately asked Paula to get the stinger out.

The sight of a woman kneeling next to her playing partner's bare bottom was simply too much for the group playing behind them.

The group raced up to the two lady golfers and asked, "Anything we can do to help?"

A young woman got on a bus, with both of her trouser pockets full of golf balls, and sat down next to a hunky guy.

The guy kept looking quizzically at her and the strange bulge.

Finally, after another few glances from him, she said to him, "It's golf balls."

The guy looked at her compassionately and said, "You poor thing. I bet that hurts a lot more than tennis elbow."

Two couples were enjoying a competitive, best ball match, wives against husbands with the losers buying lunch.

On the final hole, the match was even and one of the wives had a long, breaking, twenty foot putt to win the match. She lined the ball up carefully and confidently stroked the winning putt.

It was right on line, but unfortunately, it stopped a few inches short of the hole.

Her husband laughed and said, "Right train, wrong ticket."

The wife failed to see the humor and not cracking a smile replied, "No sleeper cars on that train either."

Two lesbians are playing together and on the 13th tee one of them hits her ball down the right and one hooks her ball into a flowerbed along the left of the fairway.

She decides to play out of the flowerbeds rather than take a drop. She takes a few practise swings, each time knocking the top off some of the buttercups, and when she hits her ball she does the same.

As she tramples out of the flowerbed destroying a few more buttercups, a fairy appears and says, "You have damaged Mother Nature. As your punishment, from now on whenever you taste butter, you will get nauseous which will serve to remind you of these buttercups you have destroyed."

The lesbian looks over at her partner across the fairway, and screams at the top of her voice, "Take a drop. Do NOT play out of the pussywillows."

Four married guys were out golfing. While playing the ninth hole, the following conversation took place:

Chris says, "You have no idea what I had to do to be able to come out golfing this weekend. I had to promise my wife that I will paint the spare room next weekend."

Derek says, "That's nothing, I had to promise my wife I will build a patio."

Bryan says, "Man, you both have it easy. I had to promise my wife I will re-do the kitchen for her."

Roy says, "You were lucky. I set my alarm for 6:30 a.m. and when it went off, I gave the wife a gentle nudge and said, 'golf course or intercourse?'"

She said, "Wear your sweater."

Whilst out on the course, two work colleagues were discussing the sexy new manager at their company.

Sally said, "I went back to his place last weekend and we had some great sex. He is much better in bed than my husband."

Emma said, "I went back to his place just two days ago, and we had sex as well, but I still think your husband is better in bed."

Two ladies came to a difficult par 3.

The first lady hits her shot straight and the ball finishes in the middle of the green.

The second lady takes a solid swing and her ball lands on the green too and it finishes just one centimeter from the first ball.

The other lady says, "Wow. I've never seen two balls so close before."

Chapter 6: Overheard on the Golf Course

Golf is the most fun you can have without taking your clothes off.

It takes me 17 holes to get warmed up.

I go into the woods so often, I can tell you which plants are edible.

Half of golf is fun. The other half is putting.

Why is it that when you tell yourself, "Don't hit it into the water," you only hear the word 'water'?

I normally manage to keep my ball in the fairway – I'm just not choosy about which fairway.

I'm convinced the reason most people play golf is to wear clothes they wouldn't normally be seen dead in.

My favorite shots are the practice swing and the conceded putt.

No matter how badly you are playing, it is always possible to play worse.

One good shank deserves another.

You think I'm a poor driver? Just wait until you see me putt.

Why am I using a new putter? Because the last one didn't float very well.

A good thing about the rain in Scotland is that most of it ends up as Scotch.

I'm hitting the woods just great, but I'm having a terrible time getting out of them.

The only time my prayers are never answered is on the golf course.

For me, one birdie is a hot streak.

I play golf with friends, but there are no such things to me as friendly games.

Golf is flog spelled backwards.

The older I get, the better I used to be.

There are two things you can do with your head down - play golf and pray.

My best score is 97, but I've only been playing for ten years.

Chapter 7: Golf Anecdotes

Golf is an odd game. You hit down to make the ball go up. You swing left and the ball goes right. The lowest score wins. On top of all that, the winner buys the drinks.

I once played with a lady captain who, after she missed a short putt, told me it was because her ball was scared of the dark.

A female golfer is often a confused soul who talks about men when she's playing golf, and about golf when she's with a man.

Golf is the only sport where the most feared opponent is yourself.

No matter how badly you play, it is always possible to get worse.

Golf is by far the ultimate love / hate relationship.

If you find golf relaxing, you're not doing it right.

Golf is like marriage. Both are expensive and if you take yourself too seriously, you're in trouble.

Golf is a hard game to work out. One day you'll slice and shank the ball and hit into lots of bunkers. The next day you go out and for no reason at all you will be completely useless.

The position of your hands is very important when playing golf. I use mine to cover up my scorecard.

A good golf partner is one who's always slightly worse than you.

A 'gimme' can best be defined as an agreement between two golfers; neither of whom can putt very well.

Golf is the ideal thing to do on Sunday because you always end up praying a lot.

A bad day at golf is better than a good day at work.

White And Dimpled

In my hand I hold a ball,
White and dimpled, rather small
Oh, how bland it does appear,
This harmless looking little sphere.

By its size I could not guess,
The awesome strength it does possess
But since I fell beneath its spell,
I've wandered through the fires of Hell.

My life has not been quite the same,
Since I chose to play this game
It rules my mind for hours on end,
A fortune it has made me spend.

It has made me curse and cry,
I hate myself and want to die
It promises a thing called "par",
If I can hit it straight and far.

To master such a tiny ball,
Should not be very hard at all
But my desires the ball refuses,
And does exactly as it chooses.

It hooks and slices, dribble and dies,
Or disappears before my eyes
Often it will have a whim,
To hit a tree or take a swim.

With miles of grass on which to land,
It finds a tiny patch of sand
Then has me offering up my soul,
If it will just drop in the hole.

It's made me whimper like a pup,
And swear that I will give it up
And take a drink to ease my sorrow,
But "The Ball" knows - I'll be back tomorrow.

Chapter 8: Golf Slang

Golfers can be quite creative when describing some of their shots, or their partner's shots. Try and remember some of these for when you are out on the course.

Slang - Tee Shots

A Sally Gunnell	Ugly to look at, but a good runner
A Forrest Gump	Keeps on running
A Glenn Miller	Didn't make it over the water
An O.J. Simpson	Got away with it
A Princess Grace	Should have taken a driver
A Princess Diana	Shouldn't have taken a driver
A Condom	Safe but unsatisfying
A Posh Spice	Too thin
A Danny DeVito	Short and fat
A Pavarotti	Sounded great but died
A Lindsay Lohan	Started straight but bent into the rough
A Jean-Marie Le Pen	Too far right
A Kerry Katona	High
An Obi-Wan Kenobi	Out of bounds

Slang - On The Course

A Simon Cowell	Needs to be hit really hard
An O.J. Simpson	Blame the golf glove
A Kate Moss	A bit thin
A Circus Tent	A big top
A Marc Bolan	Hit a tree
A Yasser Arafat	Ugly and in the sand
A Beyoncé	Chunky but on the dance floor
A Roseanne Barr	Fat and short
A Bin Laden	In the water, lost forever
A Tommy Sheridan	A shocking lie
A Dead Sheep	Still ewe
Tee Way Back	Chinese for a long hole
A Ladyboy	Looks like an easy hole but all is not what it seems

Slang - Putting

A James Joyce	A difficult read
A J. R. Tolkien	A great read
Salman Rushdie	An impossible read
A Ray Charles	Didn't see the break
A Bon Jovi	Half way there
An Elton John	A big bender
A Cuban	Needed another revolution
A Rock Hudson	Thought it was straight but it wasn't
A Danny DeVito	An ugly little five footer
A Maradona	A nasty little five footer

You're dancing, but there's no music playing...You're on the green but a long way from the flag.

Slang - In A Hazard

An Adolf Hitler	Two shots in a bunker
An Eva Braun	Picked up in a bunker
A Saddam Hussein	Go from bunker to bunker
A Red October	Underwater
A Bigfoot	Stumbling out of the woods
A Chuck Berry	Blocked out
	no particular place to go

Slang - Scoring

A Snowman	8 shots on a hole
A Beethoven	9 shots on a hole

A Spaniard   Four for four
(Stableford - 4 strokes for 4 points)

About The Author

Charlotte Croker is the niece of international best-selling author Chester Croker. Chester the Jester, as he has known, has taken Charlotte under his wing, and has been helping her re-turf her local golf course with all the divots she has taken since taking up the game.

If you have seen anything wrong in this book, or have a joke you would like to see included in the next version of the book, please visit the glowwormpress.com website and send me a message.

If you enjoyed the book, please review it on Amazon so that other female golfers can have a good laugh too.

Thanks in advance

Charlotte

The final word:-

Let's remember that golf is a game invented by the same people who think that music comes out of a bagpipe.

Made in the USA
San Bernardino, CA
23 November 2019